GOUGH WHITLAM

PROJECT TEAM

Patrick Gallagher, concept
John Iremonger and Rebecca Kaiser, captions
Geoffrey Browne and Rebecca Kaiser, pictorial research
Tabitha King and Emily O'Neill, designers
with assistance from John Faulkner, Michael Sexton, Peter Cochrane

THANKS

Rob Francis, Ian Duncan, Robyn Benjamin and the Whitlam Institute

GOUGH WHITLAM

A TRIBUTE

WITH A FOREWORD BY JOHN FAULKNER

1916–2014

First published in Australia in 2014

Allen & Unwin
83 Alexander Street
Crows Nest NSW 2065
Australia
Phone: (61 2) 8425 0100
Fax: (61 2) 9906 2218
Email: info@allenandunwin.com
Web: www.allenandunwin.com

Cataloguing-in-Publication details are available from the National Library of Australia
www.trove.nla.gov.au

ISBN 978 1 86508 437 4

Printed and bound in Australia by Ligare Pty Ltd

10 9 8 7 6 5 4 3 2 1

All royalties from the sale of this book are being donated to the Whitlam Institute.

Information on the institute can be found at www.whitlam.org

'We are like dwarves sitting on the shoulders of giants. We see more, and things that are more

distant, than they did, not because our sight is superior or because we are taller then they,

but because they raise us up, and by their great stature add to ours.'

John of Salisbury *(12th century)*

FOREWORD

Of all Australian prime ministers, Gough Whitlam was best suited to a pictorial biography, to having his life told in pictures.

The camera loved him—and he loved the camera.

Elegant and magisterial, Gough was the foremost politician of Australia's modern media age. His success, with the Labor Party and with the public, was due at least in part to his towering media presence as well as his dominating intellect and tireless enthusiasm for the Labor cause.

Inevitably, the most easily recognisable images of Gough are of him as Labor leader and then Prime Minister—silver-haired, imperiously posed, quick with a riposte or a classical allusion, bestriding the Australian political landscape. It is pictures of this Gough that instantly evoke the iconic images of Australian political history, images that encapsulate both the many achievements of his life and the moments of high drama: Gough addressing the tumultuous 1967 Victorian ALP Conference; Gough confidently announcing 'It's Time' to a rapturous audience at Blacktown Civic Centre in 1972; Gough pouring sand into the hand of Vincent Lingiari; Gough surrounded by microphones on the steps of Parliament House on the afternoon of the Dismissal.

These images captured the public imagination. They have endured because when you look at them you can almost feel the energy and dynamism Gough brought to politics.

But—as this book reminds us—Gough Whitlam was more than three years of government and three months of crisis. Here we see the familiar form of Whitlam in many circumstances that might be *unfamiliar*: standing with his flight crew in Gove (best dressed in the tropics), as a backbencher, as a son, and as a father. The pictures collected for this book illuminate the breadth and depth of Gough's life.

As a Labor Party activist, I was particularly struck by the shots that illustrate the myriad mundane tasks that must be done even by a politician of such manifold destiny as Gough—the campaign functions, public meetings, school fetes. Such time-consuming necessities are overlooked by historians and commentators eager to skip to the real story—the election win, the foreign policy decisions, the legislative tour-de-force. In this book, we can see for ourselves the work in the community that makes those moments of high drama possible.

Perhaps, inevitably, our public figures appear in our national remembrance reduced to a few simple and iconic moments. To the Australian public, Gough Whitlam is the 'It's Time' prime minister; the prime minister who swept away

23 years of conservative government; the prime minister of free education, universal health care, women's liberation, Aboriginal land rights, and the final withdrawal from Vietnam. These achievements are matched by the enduring power of the drama of the Dismissal, of instantly recognisable images of the front steps at Old Parliament House, of 'maintain the rage' and 'Kerr's cur'.

But Gough was more than this. To the Labor Party, he was our longest serving Federal leader, a talented and dedicated politician who spent twenty years on the backbench, the frontbench and in the leadership working to reform Labor's structures and policies. Rarely patient, sometimes reckless, always persistent, Gough cajoled and nudged and occasionally bludgeoned internal ALP structures into a form that could take the party to victory.

This book was the brainchild of a man who believed in Whitlam's Labor, John Iremonger. He planned its production for many years. It was a last grand project—to celebrate the life and work of Gough Whitlam.

John Iremonger died in August 2002. The team he nurtured at Allen & Unwin, led by Rebecca Kaiser, has seen this vision through.

Senator John Faulkner

An influential relationship. Gough was five years old when his father became Deputy Commonwealth Crown Solicitor and twenty when Harry Frederick Ernest Whitlam became Commonwealth Crown Solicitor. This 'discreet and self-effacing man, a model of public service propriety' left an indelible mark on his only son—a deep-seated and lifelong curiosity, a love of books and history, racial and religious tolerance, and a concern for equality. All this in the circumstances of a normal family life. As one of Gough's closest observers was to write, 'of the outstanding Labor leaders … Whitlam is the most normal in the sense that there is the smallest gap between his background and his attainments'.

Eyes to the future. Gough, without blazer, in a class photograph from his years at Sydney's Knox Grammar before the family's move to Canberra. Knox emphasised languages and the humanities, so when Gough arrived in Canberra it seems he was 'hopelessly behind' in mathematics. From his experience of being 'mucked about', he later drew the lesson that there should be a more standardised system of schooling in Australia. *(Courtesy of News Limited)*

Firmly in the middle class. Gough was eleven when the family moved from Sydney to Red Hill in Canberra, and nineteen when he went off to St Paul's College, Sydney University. The very middle-class house in very provincial Canberra was jammed with books, an ideal environment for the adolescent boy. *(Courtesy of News Limited)*

The thespian. During his four years at Canberra's Telopea Park High School, Gough became treasurer of the school's dramatic society and took the lead role in the school play. At St Paul's College, Sydney University, he continued his acting career and appeared in Ken Hall's film *The Broken Melody* (above) as a bit player. He also edited the college magazine and the Students' Representative Council magazine, captained the college debating team and was college librarian. *(Courtesy of News Limited)*

Romance. A year before meeting Margaret Dovey, the impeccably turned out Gough toasts a touring violinist, Gulia Bustabo. On her return to Europe, Ms Bustabo sent Gough a necktie from Paris. The melody may have lingered but the affair ended. *(Courtesy of News Limited)*

And then there was Margaret. Margaret Dovey, daughter of a high-achieving barrister, represented Australia as a sixteen-year-old at the Empire Games in 1938. The SCEGGS Darlinghurst schoolgirl had won an Australian championship for the 220-yards breaststroke and set a junior NSW 100-yards record. At Sydney University, theatre replaced sport as a prime interest. In 1939, at a Christmas cocktail party, the 19-year-old social work student met the law student Gough Whitlam. *(Courtesy of News Limited)*

Society wedding. 'I'm sick of this mucking about, so let's get hitched' may have been a somewhat informal way of proposing marriage, but the wedding of Gough Whitlam and Margaret Dovey on 22 April 1942 at St Michael's, Vaucluse, had all the hallmarks of a very formal affair. The press reported: 'MARRIAGE OF KC'S DAUGHTER', 'CLASSICAL GOWN FOR WEDDING'. As was the custom, the bride got all the attention. Gough was referred to as a final-year law student and member of the RAAF Reserve. *(Signing the registry courtesy of News Limited; outside the church courtesy of the Herald and Weekly Times)*

War calls. On the day the Japanese attacked Pearl Harbor, Gough joined the RAAF Reserve as an aircrew navigator. According to Gough, 'They usually put in uni types as navigators—there was no better reason'. Five months later, just after his wedding, he was called up and served three years at Gove in the Northern Territory and in the Philippines. He saw action on a number of occasions. *(Courtesy of the Whitlam Institute)*

On leave. Gough and Margaret with their first child, Anthony. The family lived for a time with Margaret's parents until Gough was discharged from the RAAF in 1945 and then returned to university to complete his law degree. *(Courtesy of the Herald and Weekly Times)*

Cronulla, 1951. Gough and his three sons on the front steps of the Whitlam home, Wangi Avenue, Cronulla. Gough joined the Labor Party in 1945, while on leave from the RAAF, a decision prompted by his support of the Curtin government's referendum to increase federal powers for post-war reconstruction. He was outraged by the cynical and spurious arguments proffered against the 'yes' case by Robert Menzies. Within two years Gough had become minute secretary for the Darlinghurst Branch and a Labor candidate for the Sydney City Council election, which was subsequently postponed. In 1947 the family moved to Cronulla. A year later, Gough unsuccessfully stood as a Labor candidate for Sutherland Shire Council. A lifetime of campaigning had begun. *(Courtesy of the Herald and Weekly Times)*

Learning the ropes. Without factional support, and with the added disadvantage of a distinctly 'silvertail' appearance, preselection was a hard slog. Nevertheless, two years after his defeat in the council election, Gough was preselected in 1950 as the Labor candidate for the state seat of Sutherland. He was unsuccessful again. Here, Gough addresses the party faithful in a suburban backyard. *(Courtesy of the National Archives of Australia)*

AUSTRALIAN LABOR PARTY
WERRIWA BY-ELECTION: NOV. 29

LIVERPOOL TOWN HALL
TUESDAY, NOVEMBER 25:

DR. H. V. EVATT
HON. E. J. WARD
E. G. WHITLAM

Censure Menzies and Fadden on three years' Mis-
management.

Restore Employment and Prosperity for all.

Preserve our Social Services and our Public Assets.

Demand Money for Homes, School and Hospitals.

E. G. WHITLAM,
B.A., LL.B.,
BARRISTER,
Ex-R.A.A.F. Air Crew.

Vote (1) WHITLAM
EDWARD GOUGH.

Authorised by T. J. FITZPATRICK, 104 Fairview Road, Cabramatta.

Federal candidate, 1952. Despite failure at council and state elections, Gough won preselection for the federal seat of Werriwa to succeed H.P. Lazzarini on his retirement. Lazzarini died in harness. In the ensuing by-election Gough gained a 12 per cent swing, and trebled his predecessor's majority. *(Courtesy of the Whitlam Institute)*

Cathy's christening, 1954. This was also the year of the Petrov Affair and the Royal Commission into Espionage. Robert Menzies used Cold War rhetoric to narrowly return the Liberal and Country Party coalition government to office. The following year the Labor Party split itself apart and the Democratic Labor Party was formed. Menzies returned to the polls once again. Despite the Coalition's crushing win, Gough's constituency support had hardened the foundation for his progress within the party. *(Courtesy of the Herald and Weekly Times)*

Leaving Cronulla. With a change of boundaries for Werriwa at the 1955 election, the Whitlams left the Sutherland Shire and moved to Cabramatta, an urban frontier in Sydney's southwest. Gough's experience of Sutherland and Cabramatta prompted a lifelong interest in urban policy, which became one of his key reform agendas, the lynchpin being 'the recognition of the distinctive and difficult character of life in the post-war suburbs of Australian cities'. He never strayed from these concerns, first expressed in his maiden speech to parliament on 19 March 1953.

I consider that I can speak with authority on that subject, because I represent an electorate that has grown very rapidly … The figures are impressive when one realises that at the re-distribution of electoral boundaries in 1948 the number on the rolls was 38,000. At the end of 1949 it was 46,000 and at the end of last year it was about 57,500. Those figures show an astonishing growth of population. The electors of Werriwa are mostly people from the inner city area who have moved to the periphery of the city, where they had hoped to be able to erect homes in more pleasant, congenial and spacious surroundings. As a result of lack of loan moneys they are without homes. Many of them are still living in the garages they built as a temporary measure. They are without hospital and high school facilities. I think it can be truthfully said that those outer suburbs have the highest birth-rate in the State.

Three 250-bed hospitals were planned at Fairfield, Liverpool and Sutherland in my electorate, but the contracts have been cancelled. No one in public life would venture to say that any of these hospitals is other than a necessity … No high schools are being erected in the electorate, and as a consequence children have to undergo the tedium and hazards of up to twenty miles travel each way to a school on five days a week …

The decline in popularity of the Government is not due merely to the evaporation of their financial reserves … It is due to the disillusion and frustration of thousands of Australians, particularly young ones who want to raise families under decent Australian and British conditions. It is clear that the people of Australia want a better deal. It is no less clear that they deserve a better deal.

(Photo courtesy of the Whitlam Institute)

The first nomination received for the Division of Werriwa was that of the sitting Labor Member, Mr. E. G. Whitlam.

Mr. Whitlam has represented the electorate of Werriwa since the by-election in November 1952 following on the death of the Hon. H. P. Lazzarini.

He was admitted to the New South Wales Bar in 1947. He had interrupted the LL.B. course to serve in the R.A.A.F. as crew from which he was discharged as a Flight Lieutenant. He graduated B.A. in 1938.

Despite having three young sons and a baby daughter, Mrs. Whitlam actively participates in her husband's activities in the electorate which, until the recent distribution, was by far the most populous in New South Wales

AUSTRALIAN LABOR PARTY

For War Pensions and social services at pre-Menzies value
Home-building loans on 5% deposit and at 3% interest.
Indirect taxation off home furniture and equipment.
Telephones for the 3,000 waiting subscribers in Werriwa.
Loan funds to complete the Shire Hospital and schools.
Abolition of the means test on allowances to the aged.
Maximum development and protection of Australia

Block

E.G. WHITLAM, B.A., LL.B., EX-RAAF

V O T E | 1 | WHITLAM, M.P. for WERRIWA

T O-N I G H T, Thursday 13th, at Miranda School of Arts
Hear E. G. WHITLAM, M.P., and T. W. DALTON, M.L.A.

A portent? Gough's nomination for the 1955 federal election was received on 11 November 1955, exactly twenty years before his government was dismissed by the governor-general. *(Courtesy of the Whitlam Institute)*

Campaigning begins. Artwork for advertisements run in local newspapers during the 1955 campaign continued the themes raised in his 1953 maiden speech. *(Courtesy of the Whitlam Institute)*

Two for the price of one. Despite the demands of four children, Margaret always actively supported Gough's political life. Here they are at the opening of a Coles New World supermarket in the heart of Werriwa. *(Courtesy of the Whitlam Institute)*

Date	Hour	Aircraft Type and No.	Pilot	Duty	REMARKS (including results of bombing, gunnery, exercises, etc.)	Flying Times	
					Time carried forward :—	1022·45	182·05
						Day	Night
4 1.6.56	0845	VH-TAS		CV	CANBERRA-MASCOT	.45	
5 6.6.56	1645	VH-TAV		DC3	MASCOT-CANBERRA	.30	.45
3 7.6.56	2155	VH-AEY	"	CANBERRA-MASCOT		1.00
8 12.6.56	0010	VH-AES	"	MASCOT-CANBERRA	1.25	
2 15.6.56	1645	VH-TAL	"	CANBERRA-MASCOT	.30	.30
3 18.6.56	1845	VH-TAN	"	MASCOT-CANBERRA		1.20
22.6.56	0925	VH-AEP	"	CANBERRA-MASCOT	1.00	
11.7.56	0800	VH-TVB	V	MASCOT-ESSENDON	1.40	
14.7.56	1920	VH-TVC	V	ESSENDON-MASCOT		1.30
19.7.56	1210	VH-TVJ	V	MASCOT-WEST BEACH	2.40	
	1640	VH-TAJ	DC3	WEST BEACH-LEIGH CREEK	1.00	1.10
	1910	"	"	LEIGH CREEK-ALICE SPRINGS		3.40
21.7.56	0955	VH-AHI	DH89	ALICE SPRINGS-HAASTS BLUFF	1.35	
	1415	"	"	HAASTS BLUFF-NARWIETOOMA	.40	
	1525	"	"	NARWIETOOMA-ALICE SPRINGS	1.05	
2.8.56	1435	"	"	VICTORIA RIVER DOWNS-MONTEJINNI	.40	
	1520	"	"	MONTEJINNI-KATHERINE	1.35	
5.8.56	1420	A65-109	DC3	DARWIN-BATHURST Is MISSION	.25	
	1630	"		BATHURST Is MISSION-DARWIN	1.15	
7.8.56	0610	VH-TAA	DC4	DARWIN-MT ISA	3.45	.30
11.8.56	0935	VH-TAO	CY	TOWNSVILLE-EAGLE FARM	2.50	
					TOTAL TIME	1046·05	192·30

A win for Werriwa. By the time Gough retired as member for Werriwa, many of the hospitals and schools he demanded for his electorate had been built. Here he joins other dignitaries, including state Minister for Education Bob Heffron, at the opening of a school in the 1950s. *(Courtesy of the Whitlam Institute)*

A humble ex-airman. From his first flight as a member of the RAAF Reserve, Gough kept a meticulous record in RAAF log books of all of his air travel. June, July and August 1956 were busy months in the sky. *(Courtesy of the Whitlam Institute)*

The local member. The duties required of Gough as a member of parliament, here at a dinner at Wentworth RSL, did not get in the way of his ambition to become deputy leader of the federal Labor Party. After being convinced by Lance Barnard on 11 November 1959 to stand for the deputy leadership, Gough finally made his tilt in 1960 when, in a close contest, he beat the 'favourite', leftwinger Eddie Ward. *(Courtesy of the Whitlam Institute)*

Thirty-six faceless men, 1963. When Gough was elected as deputy to Arthur Calwell, leader of the federal Labor Party, neither man was entitled to be a delegate to Federal Conference, the party's highest governing body. The exclusion of the leader and his deputy from its 1963 meeting led Menzies to dub the conference the 'thirty-six faceless men'. Shortly afterwards, Menzies called another early election using state aid for non-government schools, one of the issues dividing the ALP, as the trigger. The Coalition was returned with an increased majority. The Labor Party's national organisation was clearly an electoral issue, prompting Gough to begin the long and complex battle to reform its decision-making apparatus. *(Courtesy of News Limited)*

Sour relations. Relations between Whitlam and Calwell (shown here in 1965) were never close and slowly deteriorated. After four years as deputy, Gough tried to get Calwell to retire voluntarily within an agreed time. He was rebuffed. Calwell began to cultivate the Left to strengthen his position and destroy Whitlam. *(Courtesy of News Limited)*

Respite from the struggle? In January 1965 Gough took the family to New Zealand for a holiday. But tensions within the ALP were further heightened when, in an unguarded and widely reported moment, he remarked to a journalist in New Zealand that the party was in the hands of someone 'too old and weak' to lead the country. This was also the year Gough achieved notoriety in the House after he terminated a heated exchange by dousing the Liberal Paul Hasluck with a glass of water. *(Courtesy of News Limited)*

A dysfunctional partnership. Here Gough acknowledges his leader at a 1965 Caucus dinner marking Calwell's 69th birthday, 50th year in the Labor Party and 25th year in Parliament. Among the books presented to Calwell were B.A. Santamaria's *The Price of Freedom* and Vere Gordon Childe's *How Labor Governs.* Despite the gift-giving and formal accolades, the leader and his deputy were now at permanent loggerheads. *(Courtesy of News Limited)*

A suburban life. The Whitlam family lived in a modest house at 32 Albert Street, Cabramatta, until Gough was elected prime minister in 1972. This was an 'architect-designed, double frontage, flat-roofed family residence' covering 28 squares, 'including a generous outdoor patio at the back and an attached carport on the side'. While Gough was in the midst of the party-room battle for the leadership, Margaret taught swimming at the local pool and was known as a generous neighbour, bundling local kids into the back of the car for lifts to school or the station. *(Courtesy of News Limited)*

Another election, 1966. And another fierce round of campaigning, this time in the electorate of Hume. Gough visited Junee, Yass, Gundagai and Young to spruik the importance of infrastructure investment in the region. *(Courtesy of the Whitlam Institute)*

Unequal contest. Here the deputy leader faces federal treasurer, Billy McMahon, in a televised debate during the November 1966 election. Six years later, the two men would go head to head again—this time as leader of the Opposition and prime minister. In 1966, deep divisions within the Labor Party enabled the Coalition to score a landslide victory. Gough stood at the centre of those divisions. His support of state aid for non-government schools, his comment that the National Executive comprised 'twelve witless men' (which resulted in his near expulsion from the party) and his refusal to endorse his leader's policy calling for 'immediate and unconditional withdrawal' from Vietnam were a gift to the media—and the Coalition. *(Courtesy of News Limited)*

Generations of silvertails. In February 1967, on Calwell's retirement, Gough narrowly won the leadership of the Labor Party with the help of Lance Barnard, who became his deputy. The same month, three generations convened to witness Tony Whitlam gain admission to the NSW Bar. In this picture are the new leader of the Opposition Gough Whitlam, Tony Whitlam, NSW Chief Justice Sir Leslie Herron, and Tony's grandfather Mr Justice Dovey, who moved his admission. Images such as this reinforced the view widely held among sections of the ALP that Gough was a 'silvertail'. On the other side of politics, he was dubbed a 'class traitor'. *(Courtesy of News Limited)*

Among the constituents. Face to face with the voters at a trade union picnic, Gough spreads the message. Some members of his audience are less impressed than others. One of Gough's tasks was to judge the beauty contest. *(Courtesy of News Limited)*

Perils of leadership, 1967. In a life seemingly devoid of interest in sport, there were some things the new leader of the Opposition had to do. Here Gough is presented with a Collingwood jumper by captain Ray Gabelich after Barry Jones (state MP and Whitlam supporter) remarked that the football club was more popular than the Victorian ALP. Gough would earn his jumper. The new Whitlam/Barnard leadership team won the Corio by-election in July, finally wresting the seat from the Coalition after eighteen years. Later that year it won the Capricornia by-election and then went on to increase Labor's Senate vote by 5 per cent. Most importantly, with the help of the new federal secretary Cyril Wyndham, Gough won the right for the federal parliamentary leader to be a delegate to Federal Conference and to sit on the Federal Executive. *(Courtesy of the Herald and Weekly Times)*

The fight goes on. An obdurate opponent of Whitlam's attempts to reform the party's decision-making instruments was the Victorian Central Executive. Here Gough takes the fight to the 1967 Victorian State Conference where, accompanied by cheers, boos, claps and interjections, he flayed an influential handful. 'It is disgraceful that these men should be on an ALP Executive!' he said. He also flayed the party with a memorable address.

> We euphemise deep disasters as 'temporary setbacks'; the nearer Labor approaches electoral annihilation, the more fervently we proclaim our indestructibility. We juggle with percentages, distributions and voting systems to show how we shall, infallibly, at the present rate of progress, win office in 1998. Worse, we construct a philosophy of failure, which finds in defeat a form of justification and a proof of the purity of our principles. Certainly the impotent are pure…
>
> There is nothing more disloyal to the traditions of Labor than the new heresy that power is not important, or that the attainment of political power is not fundamental to our purposes. The men who formed the Labor Party in the 1890s knew all about power. They were not ashamed to seek it and they were not embarrassed when they won it.

(Photo courtesy of the Herald and Weekly Times)

At the White House. Gough's first overseas visit as leader of the Opposition was to the United States in June 1967. Here he joins President Lyndon Johnson on the White House lawn, flanked by Miss Rural Electrification and the National Orange Princess. Deliberately or not, Whitlam was sending a message to the party's Left that times had changed. *(Courtesy of Australian Picture Library)*

Power play. As leader, Gough continued his struggle to reform the party's structures. Here power-brokers Senator Sam Cohen, Senator Lionel Murphy and Gough (left to right) address the 1967 Federal Conference. Norman Makin, the last surviving member of the first Federal Conference (Adelaide, 1911), looks on. Gough, in fact, achieved four of his five main objectives for party reform. The fifth objective was to get direct national representation for the rank and file. This goal has still not been achieved. *(Courtesy of News Limited)*

In the lion's den. 'We hope the federal Labor leader will return a sorrier but a wiser man.' So remarked a member of the Victorian State Executive. It was a comment that could have been made by almost any one of the 437 delegates to the annual conference of the Victorian ALP, but Gough was never deterred by the prospect of a brawl. A year later, at the the 1968 Federal Executive, he reminded the party: 'I don't care how many prima donnas there are in the Labor Party, so long as I am the *prima donna absoluta!*' *(Courtesy of The Age)*

The Vietnam War at home. In October 1967 Gough addressed a Monash University teach-in, challenging the verities of the Left in its heartland. Against those demanding immediate withdrawal of Australian troops from Vietnam and support for the Viet Cong (the position of Jim Cairns, Gough's rival from the Left), Gough argued for the maintenance of the American alliance and support for the process designed to de-escalate the war. *(Courtesy of The Age)*

THE SILENCE
OF A LEADER

A HALF-SMILE on his lips, Mr Whitlam leaves yesterday's conference. But he refused to comment.

DAZZLED BY CAMERA flashlights, he heads for his car, still not saying a word . . .

HOUNDED by questioners, he keeps on walking.

SAFE IN HIS CAR, Mr Whitlam's half-smile returns as he is driven away.

Crisis point. *The Australian*'s page-one headline announced 'WHITLAM QUITS IN POWER GAMBLE'. At the April 1968 meeting of the Federal Executive, Gough failed to prevent the removal of right-wing Tasmanian delegate Brian Harradine. In a do-or-die effort to assert his authority, Gough announced he would resign from the leadership of the party at the end of the month. Far from receiving a vote of confidence, he faced a contest for leadership from Jim Cairns, a contest he barely managed to win by 38 votes to 32. Here Gough is followed out of the meeting by a young Bob Hogg, future federal secretary of the party. Newspapers had a field day. *(Courtesy of the Herald and Weekly Times)*

Facing the voters. Essendon Airport workshop employees provide a sceptical audience during the 1967 Senate election campaign at which Labor increased its vote. *(Courtesy of The Age)*

Art Exchange, July 1968. 'That looks like Bolte [the conservative Victorian premier]... It can't be,' Gough proclaimed. 'It's too modern.' The less imperious air Gough adopted in party politics, at least for a period after the leadership spill, appeared not so evident at this art school awards night. *(Courtesy of The Age)*

Let bygones be bygones? In early 1969, a year after Jim Cairns came close to wresting the leadership from him, Gough opened Cairns' campaign for the seat of Lalor. Between the two former protagonists, a jovial Senator Lionel Murphy. *(Courtesy of The Age)*

That man's got rhythm? After victory in the 1969 Bendigo by-election came a federal conference without major turbulence. Here the leader of the Opposition mixes it on the dance floor at the Labor Ball. *(Courtesty of the Herald and Weekly Times)*

Don's Party. In the October 1969 election, Gough led a campaign that yielded seventeen seats and a swing of 7.5 per cent to Labor. The party was readying itself for office. It was also an election that yielded David Williamson's play (and later, film) *Don's Party*. Robert Drewe, writing for *The Age*, attended the election night party at the Whitlam residence in Cabramatta.

It had been a long hard weekend. The lounge carpet showed evidence of Cabramatta's most successful party since the motor dealers' 1966 Christmas party at Sid's Restaurant and Reception Centre on the Hume Highway.

The closely trimmed back lawn had been trampled by hundreds of feet which had eagerly and nervously shifted position before a battery of television sets. The host apologised for being out of beer and lavatory paper.

He reclined on the couch with a weak scotch and a cup of coffee, looking, surprisingly, both efficient and casual at once in crisp, white shirt, striped tie, slacks and sandals.

Sunday night at 32 Albert Street, Cabramatta, and 'the leader', as Edward Gough Whitlam is known there, was completely at ease. He thinks he may be the next Prime Minister of Australia.

The night before he had greeted Labor Party helpers, neighbours and friends with warm handshakes at the front door.

'How are you? We're having a very suburban evening here,' he laughed. 'Kegs of beer on the back lawn under the Hills hoist.'

Mini-skirted campaign assistants, short-back-and-sides unionists, keen-eyed Young Turks nursed beers and stood transfixed as the television tally men first told of the strong swing to Labor.

They stood silent, almost unbelieving at first. Then a man from the Liverpool ALP branch called: 'You beauty.' Everyone cheered.

Mrs Margaret Whitlam, hospitable and radiant, denied nervousness as the competition became more tense. 'I'm not the slightest bit nervous. I always bumble along like this. But I do pour a mean beer, if I do say so myself.'

Two of the four Whitlam children—Tony, a 25-year-old giant, and Catherine, 15—moved from TV set to TV set, greeting each promising result with quiet smiles.

'The leader's got it in the bag,' said Tony at one stage. 'There's a swing of 8 $1/2$ per cent.'

'Is that good?' asked Mrs Whitlam. 'Anyway, as long as I can play golf tomorrow.'

While TV sets blared and freshly tapped kegs hissed in the night, Gough Whitlam sat in his tiny green-walled study, away from the excitement and celebrations, alone with a portable TV.

From time to time, he made forays out into the backyard, sipping a beer, greeting and receiving congratulations from the faithful, pausing at a TV set and exclaiming in amazement: 'We've won Forrest. Good grief.'

He shook hands with grizzled old strangers—'I met you in Broken Hill in 1958' they say, or 'Newcastle in '61'.

'Yes, I remember,' says the leader—and kissed beaming matrons.

He looked pleased and embarrassed at the cheers that sounded regularly as voting figures from his seat of Werriwa came to hand. 'It's very gratifying,' he said.

At 12.30 am a bunch of broken-voiced teenagers looking for action tried to crash the party. Tony Whitlam loomed out of the darkness, 6ft 5in. and 16 stone.

'It's not on blokes,' he said quietly and they padded away quickly down Albert Street.

By 1.00 am the vote counting was well over for the night. The tension was off for the day but there were still three kegs left and the crowd kicked on.

Clearly they were not even considering defeat. Neither, last night, was Gough Whitlam.

'It's been all very invigorating, this campaign,' he said, reclining back on his couch.

Relaxed, optimistic and confident he swapped off-the-record quips with reporters and earnestly studied news interviews with Prime Minister Gorton and himself.

'I'm not going to rush in and say we're going to win for sure,' he said. 'But I'm far from conceding defeat. I'm quietly confident.'

'Hey,' he called his wife, the Whitlam eyebrows shooting up quizzically. 'Has the Nixon telegram arrived yet?'

He was only half joking.

(Gough, courtesy of The Age; Gough and Cathy, courtesy of George Lipman/Fairfaxphotos; election night story, courtesy of Robert Drewe)

Vietnam again—and again. As support slipped away, the Liberal–Country Party redoubled its efforts to use opposition to the war in Vietnam to label Labor as unpatriotic and in thrall to left-wing extremists. In September 1970, Prime Minister John Gorton ordered the Australian National Information Bureau to take pictures of a Vietnam Moratorium rally on the lawns of Parliament House. Photos of Gough with a Viet Cong flag in the background were then tabled in parliament. The government gained little from such stunts. *(Courtesy of the Herald and Weekly Times)*

Soul brothers, reformers all. In the wake of federal intervention into the Victorian Executive, the Adelaide 1971 Federal Conference demonstrated a new-found party cohesion. Here the South Australian premier Don Dunstan (a reformer with a similar program to Whitlam), Bob Hawke (newly elected as president of the ACTU) and Mick Young (the party's federal secretary and a key Whitlam ally) join Gough in a toast to unity. *(Courtesy of News Limited)*

Crossing into China. Gough with his press secretary Graham Freudenberg, China specialist Dr Stephen FitzGerald, Mick Young and member for Dawson Rex Patterson arrive at the Hong Kong–China border on 2 July 1971. Derided and denounced by the Coalition government and the DLP, the trip proved a coup when the United States revealed that Secretary of State Henry Kissinger was in China at the same time preparing the way for President Nixon's visit. Labor was well ahead of the government in its assessment of this crucial area of foreign affairs. Gough had made a significant impact on the world stage. *(Courtesy of the Herald and Weekly Times)*

At the Great Wall. Gough with Dr Rex Patterson, the Canberra public servant, rural expert and rank outsider whose by-election victory in the Queensland rural seat of Dawson in February 1966 owed much to Whitlam's campaigning. It was Patterson's suggestion that a Labor delegation seek an invitation to visit China. This was in the wake of a cancelled Chinese grain contract prompted by provocative references about China by Australia's ambassador in Tokyo and the Coalition government's generally hostile attitude to the emerging giant. *(Courtesy of News Limited)*

Sustenance. There was scarcely a moment after Gough became leader when he wasn't campaigning. In October 1971 he was on the hustings for Race Mathews, his private secretary and the endorsed Labor candidate for the seat of Casey. Victoria presented the biggest electoral challenge for Labor, despite the major gains made in the 1969 election in the other states. Casey, in the expanding outer eastern suburbs, was one of the seats Labor had to win. Here a citizen makes a point during a brief stopover in a local hotel. *(Courtesy of The Age)*

The finer points of the game. Dandenong bricklayer Danny Hyndman imparts a few tips on the finer points of pool, a bonus for Gough while working in the Melbourne seat of Holt nine months before the 1972 election. *(Courtesy of The Age)*

Policies, policies. In late 1971, Labor embarked on a campaign to acquaint the electorate with its policy program. The phased release of its election policies was designed to prepare its supporters for the coming campaign, gain media attention and show that the party was now on the front foot. Many of the policies and initiatives were new to federal politics or involved the acceptance by the Commonwealth of new responsibilities. One of these was urban affairs. Here Gough and Tom Uren, the man given the shadow portfolio, use a boat slip on Sydney's polluted Parramatta River to highlight the effects of decades of neglect of the suburban environment. Uren, the member for Reid, a western suburbs Sydney seat, had first-hand experience of and a longstanding interest in urban issues. He was also one of Gough's factional opponents and a supporter of Dr Jim Cairns in the latter's bid to wrest the leadership from Whitlam in 1968. *(Courtesy of News Limited)*

Multi-skilling. Gough reaches the culinary heights during a Labor fund-raising picnic at the Narrabeen Fitness Camp on the northern outskirts of Sydney. Not loaves and fishes but rolls and 'snags'. All part of the requirement to demonstrate he was in touch with the rank and file. *(Courtesy of News Limited)*

Staking out rights. The 1972 election was the first in which Aboriginal issues took centre stage. In February, Gough visited the newly established 'tent embassy' outside Parliament House in response to a challenge from Aboriginal activist Paul Coe. Gough pledged that 'Labor will absolutely reverse the government's policy and allow ownership of land by tribal communities. This is something which has been accepted in international law since 1956.' Despite his best intentions, it was to take two more decades and the Mabo High Court decision for the original Australians to secure some rights to their land. *(Courtesy of News Limited)*

A potent partnership. By mid 1972 Margaret Whitlam was a practised campaigner. Here she and Gough set in motion Tony Lamb's 'action-mobile', used for his campaign in the marginal seat of La Trobe on the edge of Melbourne. Lamb won the seat in the December election. *(Courtesy of The Age)*

Other Lives. Margaret Whitlam was completing a social work diploma when she first met Gough. In 1964 she returned to part-time social work at Parramatta District Hospital and generally stayed clear of direct involvement in politics until the 1969 election campaign. In early 1972 she joined Gough on what the press chose to call 'a whistle-stop poverty tour'. It highlighted the inadequacy, lack of coordination and mean-spiritedness of the Coalition's grab-bag of welfare programs and brought attention to key policies in Labor's program. The press headline for this picture was 'HOW TO SURVIVE ON $45 A WEEK'. *(Courtesy of News Limited)*

Recalling battles of a different kind. Ex-Flight Lieutenant Whitlam and ex-Flight Lieutenant Tardent share a chinwag during the presentation of the 13 Squadron plaque at the Surfers Paradise RSL. A 'photo opportunity' during the Labor candidate Tom Vievers' campaign for the seat of McPherson. *(Courtesy of The Age)*

A degree of informality. By the time Gough shared this poolside meal with Mick Young at the Surfers Paradise meeting of the Federal Executive in October 1972, Young had the key elements of the upcoming election campaign in place. *(Courtesy of News Limited)*

A little ray of sunshine. Gough, dressed appropriately but still with a pen and sheaf of papers, working on his policy speech. He warned against over-confidence in the party: 'I don't want people to rest on their oars.' *(Courtesy of the Courier-Mail)*

Thespians all. Gough with Rudolf Nureyev and Sir Robert Helpmann on the set of the film *Don Quixote* in a hangar at Melbourne's Essendon Airport. Like Don Quixote, Gough was a pursuer of lofty ideals. *(Courtesy of The Age)*

The pay-off. Months of policy work, careful planning and the talents of Graham Freudenberg as speechwriter culminated with the opening of the 1972 federal election campaign at Blacktown's Civic Centre on 13 November. 'Men and Women of Australia!' Gough declared, 'The decision we will make for our country on 2 December is a choice between the past and the future, between the habits and fears of the past, and the demands and opportunities of the future. There are moments in history when the whole fate and future of nations can be decided by a single decision. For Australia, this is such a time. It's time for a new team, and a new program, a new drive for equal opportunities; it's time to create new opportunities for Australians, time for a new vision of what we can achieve in this generation for our nation and the region in which we live. It's time for a new government—a Labor government.'
(Courtesy of Fairfaxphotos)

The crest of a wave. The camera catches a bizarre moment at the end of the policy speech. Laurie Oakes and David Solomon wrote in their book *The Making of an Australian PM*: 'There was, of course, a standing ovation … It went on and on.' *(Courtesy of Sydney Morning Herald)*

Another view of the crowd. Gough arriving at City Square in Melbourne. Note the apparent absence of security personnel. Not for Whitlam the limo sweeping up, depositing him and then collecting him the moment his speech was over. *(Courtesy of the Herald and Weekly Times)*

Where's Whitlam? In full campaign mode during the last days of the 1972 campaign. They may not all have voted for him, but they wanted to see him in action. Years of public performance, capped off by a policy speech that was made for TV, brought out the crowds. *(Courtesy of the Herald and Weekly Times)*

It's Time. Labor fought the 1972 election with the help of a nationally co-ordinated campaign that paid special attention to television—and provided the press with an abundance of material. The It's Time slogan, the work of the first-ever National Campaign Committee, presided over by Mick Young, proved a highly effective summary of the spirit of the campaign. Labor chose the battleground, called the shots and was united, while the Liberals, under the shaky leadership of the hapless Billy McMahon, were ever on the defensive. Here Gough poses for the camera with pop star Little Pattie, one of the many performers who were part of creating arguably the country's most famous campaign jingle.

It's time for freedom,
It's time for moving, It's time to begin,
Yes It's time

It's time Australia,
It's time for moving, It's time for proving,
Yes It's time

It's time for all folk,
It's time for moving, It's time to give,
Yes It's time

It's time for children,
It's time to show them, It's time to give,
Yes It's time

Time for freedom,
Time for moving, Time to be clear,
Yes It's time

Time Australia,
Time for moving, It's time for proving,
Yes It's time

It's time for better,
Come together, It's time to move,
Yes It's time

Time to stand up,
Time to shout it, Time, Time, Time,
Yes It's time

Time to move on,
Time to stand up, time to say 'yes',
Yes It's time

(Photo courtesy of News Limited; lyrics reproduced courtesy of the ALP National Secretariat)

Images of unity. Margaret and Gough Whitlam and Bob and Hazel Hawke toast a future victory two days before election day. Hawke had become president of the ACTU in 1970 and senior vice-president of the ALP in 1971. His positive involvement in the campaigning ensured a degree of co-ordination between the industrial and political wings of the labour movement hitherto unheard of. *(Courtesy of the Herald and Weekly Times)*

Margaret and Gough vote. On 2 December 1972 the Whitlams cast their federal ballot for the thirteenth time since Gough won preselection for Werriwa in 1952. *(Courtesy of The Age)*

Victory assured. Well-wishers greet the new Prime Minister of Australia on his return to his Cabramatta home with chants of 'We want Gough'. *(Courtesy of Fairfaxphotos)*

Never-failing support. A cake had been prepared to celebrate victory, 'just in case'. Margaret and daughter Cathy offer a beaming Gough their congratulations. *(Courtesy of News Limited)*

From suburban streets to the corridors of power. Gough and Cathy return from a breakfast visit with the neighbours the day following the victory and 25 years after Gough's first campaign as Labor candidate for Sydney City Council. *(Courtesy of The Age)*

A welcome to Canberra. E.G. Whitlam, Prime Minister-elect, is greeted at Fairbairn Airbase by an enthusiastic crowd which included Kep Enderby (right), the member for the ACT soon to become a minister in the Whitlam government. *(Courtesy of the Whitlam Institute)*

Moving in. Gough and Margaret in the grounds of the Lodge in Canberra the day they moved in. This was a far cry from Albert Street, Cabramatta, their home for seventeen years. *(Courtesy of the Canberra Times)*

The birth of the duumvirate. Anxious to begin governing, Whitlam chose not to wait until Caucus was able to assemble to choose a ministry. Instead, he created a two-man government, allocating 27 portfolios to himself and deputy leader Lance Barnard. It was, as the journalist Paul Kelly pointed out, the first time since 1929 that a new Labor government had been formed as the result of an election. Here, Gough Whitlam and Lance Barnard join the Governor-General, Sir Paul Hasluck, at the swearing in. Sir Paul was a former Liberal minister and the man on the receiving end of a glass of water tossed by the then leader of the Opposition during a session of parliament in 1965. *(Courtesy of The Age)*

Duumvirs. For two weeks Gough Whitlam and Lance Barnard governed Australia in an unprecedented arrangement. As Gough remarked with characteristic erudition, 'It was the smallest government with authority over Australia since the brief Wellington administration in 1839'. Among the decisions taken during the duumvirate's thirteen days in office were: an immediate end to national service call-up; the re-opening of an equal pay case for women before the Federal Conciliation and Arbitration Court; freeing draft resisters from gaol; Australia's recognition of the People's Republic of China; an end to the granting of further leases on Aboriginal reserves; ratifying international conventions on nuclear arms, racial discrimination and labour; creating an interim committee of the Australian Schools Commission; and ending all official and commercial contacts with Rhodesia. Caucus assembled on 18 December to elect the full ministry and the duumvirate's reign was over. What powered this unprecedented activity? Gough's abundant energy (hitherto expended on endless campaigning), the expectations built around the It's Time theme, making up for a quarter century of lost opportunities and, of course, a certain glee in pointing out the indolent confusion of the previous government. *(Courtesy of The Age)*

Consistency. On their seventh day in office, the duumvirate invited the premiers of New South Wales and Victoria to discuss plans for a regional growth centre at Albury–Wodonga with Tom Uren, the soon to be appointed Minister for Urban Affairs (seated next to Gough). According to Gough: 'There was some light-hearted discussion of the naming of the new growth centre. It was thought that Uren did not lend itself to suffixes or prefixes. The premiers could not agree on Askinville or Hamerton. There was general consensus, however, on the virtues of Whitlambad.' *(Courtesy of The Age)*

The ceremonial opening of the 28th Parliament. Sharing the best seats in the House with Gough were Deputy Prime Minister Lance Barnard and the Attorney-General, Senator Lionel Murphy (right). Later Barnard was to look back on the days when he and Gough were the government: 'The public were, I think, pleased something was being done…' At Barnard's funeral in August 1997, Gough found it difficult to contain his grief: 'I honour especially the staunchness of my oldest and best mate.' *(Courtesy of News Limited)*

Dealing with the premiers. So much of the Whitlam program depended upon the support—or at least the non-obstruction—of state premiers. A great deal of effort (much of it, in the final analysis, wasted) was spent in attempting to reach a measure of federal–state consensus on issues of national concern. Here the leader of a federal government barely three months old meets state premiers Don Dunstan (SA), Robin Askin (NSW) and Rupert Hamer (Vic.) to work towards a common program to combat salinity. Despite these early discussions, salinity still remains one of Australia's great environmental challenges. *(Courtesy of News Limited)*

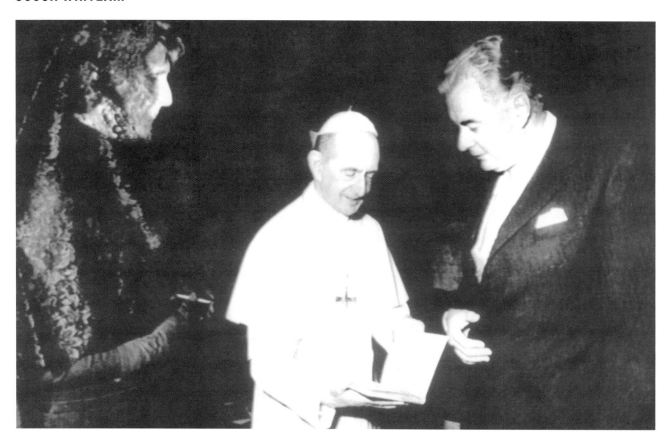

The Pontiff and the Prime Minister. Admiring the Vatican's political prowess and its active participation in United Nations specialised agencies, Gough moved quickly to establish diplomatic relations with the Holy See. He and Margaret received an audience with Paul VI in Easter week 1973. *(Courtesy of Australian Picture Library)*

Testing federalism. The first premiers conference during the Whitlam government, in June 1973, provided a test for the new activist federalism at the heart of Gough's policymaking. Queensland's premier, Joh Bjelke-Petersen, summed up an entrenched opposition: 'The Commonwealth must cease regarding all revenue as "our" money, in which it will dictate how the money will be spent by attaching strings and conditions … The Commonwealth should remember that it is a child of the States … We've seen too much in the last three months of the use of the bludgeon and the carrot.' *(Courtesy of News Limited)*

Great and powerful friends? Shortly after winning the election, Whitlam wrote to United States president Richard Nixon expressing deep concern over the breakdown of negotiations with North Vietnam and the resumption of heavy bombing. Nixon was reported to be furious at this, but in July 1973, thanks to careful work on both sides and despite spoiling tactics from the Opposition, Whitlam met Nixon in Washington. *(Courtesy of AAP Information Services)*

Looking for luck. In June 1973 Gough became the first Australian prime minister since 1959 to visit India. Here, somewhat awkwardly, he attempts to encircle the famed fourth century Ashoka pillar in Delhi. Legend has it that doing so will bring luck. *(Courtesy of Australian Picture Library)*

Federation at work. Dealing with the premiers was rarely this genial. At virtually every turn, the Whitlam program was diverted, delayed or destroyed when it required the co-operation of the states. Here Gough shares a brief peace with New South Wales' Robin Askin and Victoria's Rupert Hamer. Then it was back to the bargaining table. *(Courtesy of News Limited)*

Whitlam and Windsor. The election of the Whitlam government was seen as a great boost for the republican cause. Elizabeth II's change of title to Queen of Australia prompted Queensland ALP senior vice-president Jack Edgerton to greet her thus: 'They tell me, luv, you've been naturalised.' *(Courtesy of the Canberra Times)*

Acknowledging Japan. Successive Coalition governments had resisted overtures from the Japanese government to normalise relations. In contrast, among the many initiatives undertaken by the Whitlam government, was a State visit during which Gough and Margaret were received by Emperor Hirohito and Empress Nagako. *(Courtesy of National Archives of Australia)*

Meeting Mao. Within three weeks of his election victory, Gough reversed over two decades of policy and recognised the government of the People's Republic of China as the sole legal government of China. In November 1973 he joined his ambassador to China, Dr Stephen FitzGerald, in Beijing where they met Chairman Mao Zedong and Premier Zhou-Enlai. *(Courtesy of National Archives of Australia)*

On stage, again. Gough and Margaret were invited to the stage during a performance interlude on their historic trip to China. *(Courtesy of the National Library of Australia)*

Turning the first sod. A national gallery had been promised by the Coalition since 1965 but nothing eventuated other than muddle and rhetoric. In his 1972 policy speech Gough undertook to turn words into deeds. By November 1973, work had begun on the building. Here the first director, James Mollison, greets the Prime Minister on site. *(Courtesy of the Canberra Times)*

Populist politics. In Melbourne it is vitally important to proclaim allegiance to an Aussie Rules team. Carlton had Robert Menzies and B.A. Santamaria as members. Here, the legendary Graham 'Polly' Farmer inducts Gough Whitlam into the Geelong club. In 1967 it seemed a good idea to don a Collingwood jumper. *(Courtesy of the Herald and Weekly Times)*

A winning smile. In dramatic contrast to his predecessors, Gough enjoyed jousting with the press and it enjoyed jousting with him. The launch of *Whitlam and Frost*, a transcript of the TV interviews with the high-profile British interviewer David Frost, was one such occasion. *(Courtesy of the Canberra Times)*

A new opponent. The Liberals' successor to the hapless Billy McMahon was Billy Snedden. He proved no match for the Prime Minister, although he did perform better than expected in this televised debate in December 1973. In parliament, Gough established an early ascendancy over Snedden, who tended to confuse 'a show of toughness with strength'. *(Courtesy of News Limited)*

Campaigning, again. Australia went to the polls on 8 December 1973 to vote on the two referendums to give the Commonwealth control over prices and incomes. Despite help from loyal campaign workers such as this man in Sydney's Green Valley, both referendums were decisively defeated. *(Courtesy of the Whitlam Institute)*

Made of bronze. An uncharacteristically silent Gough Whitlam at the Melbourne office of the Australia Council. The bronze bust was the work of Julius Sasadi. *(Courtesy of The Age)*

Internationalism. Gough's interest in Australia's place in the wider world extended to his own party. Labor began to play a more prominent role in the Socialist International, a social democratic association of national parties sharing a common view. From the moment he became deputy leader, Gough made a point of meeting the heads of fraternal parties overseas. Here he talks to German chancellor, Willy Brandt, via satellite. *(Courtesy of Fairfaxphotos)*

Not happy, Gough. Gough appointed a task force led by H.C. 'Nugget' Coombs to review the multitude of assistance measures that were the legacy of the previous government. Coombs identified 141 items. The decision to remove the superphosphate subsidy paid to farmers provoked much opposition and Gough bore the brunt of it at a public meeting in Forrest Place, Perth, in March 1974. He was pelted with eggs, pies, tomatoes, sandwiches and a full can of drink. It was his rowdiest meeting yet. *(Courtesy of the West Australian)*

Hidden nemesis. 'A man in the plenitude of his powers' was Gough's description of Sir John Kerr when he announced the appointment of the new governor-general on 27 February 1974. Gough had chosen a lawyer who had built a career at the Bar on cases with considerable political significance. A one-time member of the Labor Party, Kerr had been approached by the DLP and later by Billy McMahon regarding the prospect of running for a safe Liberal seat. He was a dangerous appointment, although no one foresaw how that danger might manifest itself. Kerr, who once said 'Law is so intimately connected with the distribution, exercise and control of political power in every field', was promoted to KCMG in this ceremony on 18 April 1974 'in further recognition of his distinguished legal services'. *(Courtesy of the Sydney Morning Herald)*

Calling the bluff. At no point in its turbulent three years in government did Labor enjoy a majority in the Senate. In April 1974, barely sixteen months after the December 1972 election, Gough called Billy Snedden's bluff when the Senate voted by 31 to 26 against putting the Appropriation (Supply) Bills to the vote. Here the Prime Minister marches off to see the Governor-General on 10 April. At 8.30 pm that evening, Gough announced a double dissolution election for 18 May 1974. *(Courtesy of The Age)*

Another policy speech. In 1974 Gough chose to undertake to fulfil promises rather than chart a new course, and to challenge the Opposition to produce something new rather than let it return to the old. *(Courtesy of the Courier Mail)*

Fraternity. Gough, ACTU president Bob Hawke (right) and secretary of the NSW Labour Council John Ducker (centre) on the campaign trail. Note the ACTU president's rather more amorous grip on his glass of beer than that of Gough. *(Courtesy of The Age)*

Working with the unions. Gough's relationship with the union movement was often rocky, but the 1974 double dissolution campaign saw the emergence of ACTU president Bob Hawke as a formidable campaigner. *(Courtesy of The Age)*

Back at Blacktown. Gough delivered his policy speech for the 1974 election on 29 April at the Blacktown Civic Centre, the venue that had worked so well for him and Labor in 1972. *(Courtesy of the Whitlam Institute and Martin Brannan/Fairfaxphotos)*

Prime ministerial perks. The chance to be introduced to 'Ol' Blue Eyes' in 1974 was too good an opportunity to refuse. The meeting ended a day of by-election campaigning in the NSW state seat of Coogee. At the Coogee Sports Club, Gough was presented with a stirrer's paddle. 'I realise this is only honorary but I would like the manufacturer's name because I know so many people qualified for it.' *(Courtesy of News Limited)*

The Prime Minister meets a prophet. There may have been a mood of optimism at the 1974 Brisbane Labour Day march, but that year's election result was a long way from a resounding victory. *(Courtesy of News Limited)*

Prelude to a kiss. 'At the outset of the 1974 election campaign I was persuaded to appear at the climax of the film *Barry McKenzie Holds His Own*. In what I suppose was a cameo role, I was cast to welcome Mrs Edna Everidge (aka Barry Humphries) on her return to Sydney airport. I embellished the script by exhorting: "Arise, Dame Edna." The title has been used ever since. It was the only Imperial honour my government ever conferred.' Gough also bestowed Mrs Everidge a peck on the cheek. The press hailed the event as 'the kiss that made Australian history'. *(Courtesy of News Limited)*

Another election night party. A second victory wave, this time from a balcony at Warwick Farm in western Sydney. Labor was returned with a five-seat majority. The Senate vote saw the elimination of the DLP, but two independents held the balance of power. Post-election, Snedden declared: 'We were not defeated. We just didn't get enough seats to form a government.' *(Courtesy of Fairfaxphotos)*

Uneasy smiles. In 1967, Dr Jim Cairns challenged Gough for the leadership of the federal Labor Party, one more bout in a lengthy contest between the two. Cairns' election as Deputy Prime Minister after the May 1974 election was a reminder of that ancient rivalry and an indication that Gough Whitlam's control of Caucus was by no means complete. *(Courtesy of the Canberra Times)*

A sea of suits. After the election was declared Caucus sat down to choose a ministry. Gough had become the first Labor leader to win two successive elections, but rather than acknowledge this special status Caucus chose a basically unchanged team. The opportunity for new talent and a fresh approach was lost. *(Courtesy of News Limited)*

Back to work. The morning after Caucus elected the ministry Gough called an unofficial Cabinet meeting. The pace would not slacken despite the view among many Caucus members that the government was doing too much, too quickly without ensuring the support of the electorate for its myriad initiatives and decisions. *(Courtesy of the Canberra Times)*

A weekend chat. By 1974 Australia faced an unprecedented inflation rate and increased levels of unemployment, conditions shared by most western industrialised nations in the wake of the 1973 OPEC oil crisis. However, Australia's problems were exacerbated by the government's expansionary budget and its decision not to increase taxes to fund its program. In November 1974 the Prime Minister and the president of the ACTU met for a brief heart-to-heart discussion on unemployment. *(Courtesy of The Age)*

Rumours. Three days after Treasurer Frank Crean presented his budget on 19 August 1974, two front pages appeared in Sydney's *Sun* newspaper. The next day's *Australian* carried a lead story headed 'RUMOURS FLYING BUT WHITLAM STAYS'. The story that followed read: 'For a while, many people thought he had [quit]—it was the biggest rumour of all in what had been one of the most extraordinary Budget planning weeks ever seen in Parliament House. No one really knows how it got started, but it raced around the country so fast that Mr Whitlam was forced to deny it … Stories circulating in the upper echelons of the public service went as far as to say that Mr Whitlam had actually presented his resignation to Cabinet … One possible launching point for the rumour is thought to be Mr Whitlam's visit to Government House, but that was on Wednesday, for a routine Executive Council meeting. The apparent take-over of the Budget strategy by the Deputy Prime Minister, Dr Cairns, also seemed to give it a kick along …' *(Courtesy of Fairfaxphotos)*

Changeover time. Mounting economic woes led Gough to swap Treasurer Frank Crean (left) for Jim Cairns (right) in December 1974. Crean became Minister for Overseas Trade. Treasurer Cairns was to last less than six months, brought down by his own staff: his principal private secretary Juni Morosi and his son Philip. Administrative chaos in the Treasurer's office compounded the effect of the revelation of private and clandestine fundraising authorised from that office. *(Courtesy of the Canberra Times)*

Christmas cheer? December 1974 and Australia's ambassador to Ireland, Vince Gair, introduces Gough to Ireland's President Cearbhall O'Dalaigh. To gain an extra Senate seat for Labor at the 1974 half Senate election, Gough collaborated with Attorney-General Lionel Murphy to persuade Vince Gair, until October 1973 the DLP leader in the Senate, to resign and take up the post of Australia's ambassador to Ireland. Billy Snedden used the appointment as one of the justifications to block supply in the Senate in an effort to force an election. Gough accepted the challenge and narrowly won the double dissolution election. The legacy of the Gair affair was mixed. It destroyed the DLP, but it left Labor with the smell of backroom dealings and opportunism. And it alerted Queensland premier Joh Bjelke-Petersen to the possibilities of breaking convention and installing a puppet senator in Gair's place. *(Courtesy of Australian Picture Library)*

Darwin flattened. Gough was in Europe on a controversial five-week tour when Cyclone Tracy devastated Darwin on Christmas Eve 1974. In going ahead with the trip, Gough ignored both public criticism and the counsel of his advisors. He flew home briefly to visit those affected by the disaster but returned to Europe almost immediately after. The political fallout was enormous and, according to Graham Freudenberg, for the first time in his career 'Gough came perilously close to becoming a figure of ridicule'. *(Courtesy of National Archives of Australia)*

Not quite an Australia Day message. Gough's address to the nation, recorded on 22 January 1975, occurred in the middle of the Loans Affair in which the government was accused of using Pakistani businessman Tirath Khemlani to broker an illegal loan from the Middle East. Six days after the broadcast, Governor-General Sir John Kerr signed an authority to seek $2000 million in overseas loans 'for temporary purposes'. *(Courtesy of News Limited)*

The Gough and Bob show. Although they looked relaxed enjoying a beer at the ALP National Conference at Terrigal's Florida Hotel in February 1975, both Gough and Bob knew the year ahead would be torrid as criticism of the government's handling of the economy increased. *(Courtesy of Fairfaxphotos)*

Fallen empires, welcome respite. Here Gough and Margaret survey the Inca city of Machu Picchu during a brief holiday in April to mark their 33rd wedding anniversary. Gough's penchant for overseas trips, even when the majority were working trips to advance an activist foreign policy agenda, provided endless press comment, much of it negative. John Menadue, Gough's secretary of the Department of Prime Minister and Cabinet, wrote: 'Travel revived his sagging spirits in quite a remarkable way … Whitlam had to get away or he would have been sapped of all energy and probably destroyed.' *(Courtesy of The Age)*

Dangerous liason. Gough first visited Indonesia as Prime Minister within three months of the December 1972 victory to demonstrate the political and economic interest Australia was now taking in the region. Indonesian President Soeharto asked him to return in September 1974 and Gough invited the Indonesian President to Townsville in April 1975. It was a developing relationship for which the people of East Timor were to pay a huge price. *(Courtesy of Australian Picture Library)*

The end of a long campaign. Gough with the first prime minister of Papua New Guinea, Michael Somare, at the ceremony marking the country's independence on 15 September 1975. As long ago as 1960, Gough had urged the Australian government to provide for eventual independence. For much of that time his was a lone voice. In August 1975 Gough introduced the Bill that created the new nation of Papua New Guinea. *(Courtesy of the Herald and Weekly Times)*

Dear Caucus Member

If you were to ask me if the signature below is mine, I
would have to say "it looks very much like it".   If you
were to ask me did I sign this letter I would have to say
"I have no recollection of signing it".   Am I incompetent?
Not in possession of normal senses?   Am I non compus
mentus?   Of course not.

Today's technology allows even an amateur the capacity to
produce the most convincing misrepresentations.   The
signature below should look like mine because it is a
photocopy of my signature.   And if I cannot remember
signing it, that is understandable because I did not sign
it.

                    Yours sincerely,

                    E. G. WHITLAM

PRIME MINISTER

CANBERRA

2 JUL 1975

Dear Dr Cairns,

I have received your letter of 2 July with
its attached photostat of your letter of 10 March,
which you quoted in the House on 5 June (Hansard, page
3463), and an unsigned statement by Phillip Cairns.

You sent me these documents in response to
our discussion yesterday about, first, the photostat
copy of the letter of 7 March which, as you agreed,
appeared to bear your signature and, secondly, your
responsibility for your staff.

I do not regard these documents as satisfactory
explanations of these two issues which I put to you and
which with your consent I stated to the press.

Since you write that you do not intend to
resign from any position you hold, I must advise the
Governor-General to terminate your commission. He
will receive me at 8 o'clock this evening. I feel
that thereafter I must release copies of your documents
and of this letter to the press.

Yours sincerely,

Cairns, Connor, Whitlam. The three principal players in the Loans Affair that so dramatically eroded support for the Whitlam government meet at Canberra's Fairbairn RAAF base. *(Courtesy of the Canberra Times)*

Fakery. False signatures weren't the only bit of fakery Gough had to contend with. Crippling hostility between the government and Treasury nearly allowed fraudster Tirath Khemlani to swindle Australia out of $100 million. *(Courtesy of the Whitlam Institute)*

At loggerheads. Cairns' letter of support for a businessman's attempts to raise loan funds to finance land developments in Melbourne's western suburbs on behalf of the Australian government, and which he denied existed, contributed mightily to the air of instability and impropriety that threatened to engulf the Whitlam government. Less than two months separate the photograph of Whitlam and Cairns at Fairbairn and the letter in which Whitlam advised Cairns of his sacking. It was the beginning of a week from which the Whitlam government would never recover. *(Courtesy of the Whitlam Institute)*

Fighting for his life. At the end of the week in which Cairns was sacked, and in the face of mounting public alarm, Gough made a characteristic move. He recalled the House of Representatives from its winter recess for a special sitting. On the floor of parliament, he would be on his home ground in an all-out fight to restore the government's credibility. On 9 July 1975, the House heard Whitlam in full flight, but even his formidable oratory could not disguise the disarray at the government's very heart. The Senate, controlled by the Opposition, resolved to call key officials before it for questioning a week later. The result was a fiasco. The Opposition was unable to advance its cause and the government was unable to reverse the tide of public opinion. Gough was under siege, especially from an unrelenting media pack. *(Courtesy of The Age)*

Greek National Day Celebrations. At no point in his prime ministership did Gough lose the loyalty of Greek Australians. Australia's ethnic communities were wooed and won over many years. Only those from the Baltic states, who were fiercely anti-communist, stayed beyond the circle of admirers. *(Courtesy of The Age)*

Two warriors meet at the Colosseum. Gough derived enormous pleasure from his visits to Italy, facing the derision of his opponents—and sometimes the exasperation of his colleagues. Despite his education in the classics and love of Ancient Greek and Roman civilisations, Gough did not visit Europe until 1962, when he was 46. The intensity of his passion for visits to the principal sites of the classical world might have been seen, in part, as making up for lost time. Standing in the Forum he told John Menadue, 'Comrade, this is the most important place on earth, much more so than Jerusalem'. *(Courtesy of AAP Information Services)*

Political foes. Gough and the new leader of the Opposition, Malcolm Fraser, share a podium at the inaugural meeting of the Ethnic Communities Council of NSW on 27 July 1975. It was described as the first official confrontation between the two men. Gough spoke for nearly 40 minutes and Fraser was 'clearly piqued' by both the length and content of Gough's speech. By the end, Fraser 'had torn to shreds part of a camelia' and then rebuked Gough with a brief eight-minute reply. *(Courtesy of News Limited)*

A message from the original owners. By the advent of the 1960s, it had become clear to anyone who wanted to see that the rights of Aboriginal people could no longer be left to state governments and parliaments. Gough's 1972 policy speech succinctly stated: 'We will legislate to give Aborigines land rights—not just because the case is beyond argument, but because all of us as Australians are diminished while Aborigines are denied their rightful place in this nation.' In May 1974 the Woodward Royal Commission recommended a form of land rights for Aboriginal people. Here, in September 1975, Gough receives a message from representatives of the Mornington Island community. *(Courtesy of News Limited)*

A brief moment on a long road of struggle. Gough Whitlam pours sand into the hand of Vincent Lingiari, an elder of the Gurindji people, to symbolise the handing back of Aboriginal land by the Australian people. 'On this great day, I, the Prime Minister of Australia, speak on behalf of all Australian people—all those who honour and love this land we live in. For them I want to say to you: I want this to acknowledge that we Australians have much to do to redress the injustice and oppression that has for so long been the lot of Black Australians. Vincent Lingiari, I solemnly hand to you these deeds as proof, in Australian law, that these lands belong to the Gurindji people and I put into your hands part of the earth itself as a sign that this land will be the possession of you and your children forever.' *(Courtesy of the Canberra Times)*

Unreserved support. Within months of his elevation as leader of the Opposition, Malcolm Fraser announced the Coalition's decision to block supply. Gough resolved to treat this announcement as the first move in a battle of nerves. The main anvil on which to crack the Opposition's resolve during the supply crisis was the parliament, but campaigning among the community was an important weapon as well. Here, a newspaper caption says it all: 'Migrants at a rally in Melbourne Town Hall yesterday gave the Prime Minister one of the most enthusiastic welcomes accorded any Australian politician—men in the crowd hugged and kissed him as he arrived to speak.' *(Courtesy of The Age)*

Going their separate ways? Three weeks before the Dismissal, Gough and the Governor-General seem ready to set off on separate paths. To Gough, there were only two combatants in the struggle over supply: the government with its control of the House of Representatives, and the Opposition with its control of the Senate. Unbeknownst to him, there was also a third and decisive player, Sir John Kerr, advised by the Chief Justice Sir Garfield Barwick. *(Courtesy of News Limited)*

'Twas the night before catastrophe. On the evening of 10 November 1975, Gough attended a banquet hosted by the Lord Mayor of Melbourne, Ron Walker (who was later to become treasurer of the Liberal Party). Graham Freudenberg, Gough's speech writer and an acute observer of politics, wrote of the annual show of strength and solidarity by the Melbourne establishment 'where a Labor PM was an exhibit and an enemy.' 'These were men who, more than any other group in Australia, had put pressure on the Opposition to use their numbers in the Senate to block the Budget and bring down the Labor Government. As Whitlam in his speech gently taunted them, they listened, half hating, half admiring the nerve and style of this impossible man and were certain they had lost.' *(Courtesy of the Herald and Weekly Times)*

TUESDAY 11 NOVEMBER 1975

9.00 am	Mtg with Crean, Daly, Fraser, Lynch & Anthony
9.30 am	Caucus
11.45 am	Parliament
2.00 pm	Gov-Gen. withdrew PM's commission
2.00 pm	Parliament
5.00 pm	Mtg with G-G
5.30 pm	Parliament
5.50 pm	Press Conference
7.00 pm	Caucus
7.30 pm	CLAC

Life goes on. Gough's diary on the day of his eventful meeting with Sir John Kerr. *(Courtesy of the Whitlam Institute)*

Thunderclap. On the steps of Parliament House, 4.45 pm, 11 November 1975. David Smith, the Governor-General's secretary, reads the proclamation of dismissal over the shouts of some 2000 protesters who had flocked to Parliament House in support of the Labor government: '…now therefore I, Sir John Kerr, the Governor-General of Australia, do this by my proclamation dissolve the Senate and the House of Representatives … Given by my hand and the Great Seal of Australia, 11 November 1975. God Save the Queen.' Gough then moved to the microphone and defiantly uttered arguably the most memorable lines ever spoken in Australian politics: 'Well may we say God save the Queen, because nothing will save the Governor-General. The proclamation which you have just heard read by the Governor-General's official secretary was counter-signed Malcolm Fraser, who will undoubtedly go down in history from Remembrance Day, 1975, as Kerr's cur.' *(Courtesy of News Limited)*

Full campaign mode. Within a week of the Dismissal, Gough was on the campaign trail with rallies in Sydney, Melbourne, Hobart and Adelaide. Everywhere, he attracted bigger and louder crowds than in 1972 or 1974. The campaign opener in Sydney's Domain was the biggest political meeting the city had seen since Jack Lang's rallies during the Depression. Melbourne's Festival Hall, a few hours later, hosted an even more emotional meeting. *(Courtesy of The Age)*

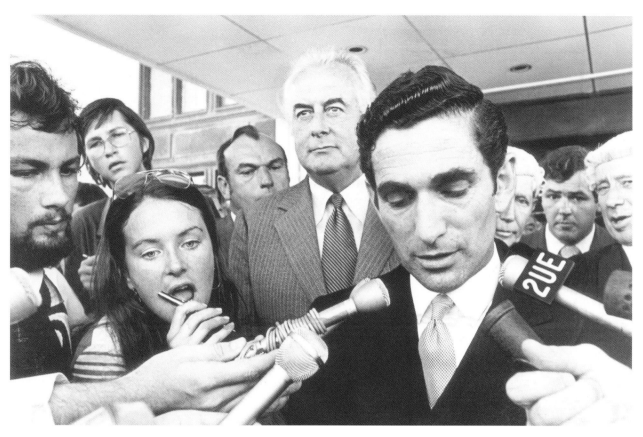

A truly hectic campaign. In Rockhampton, a presidential seal graced the podium. Back in Sydney, TV star Grahame Bond threw his support, and that of much of the Australian arts community, behind the leader. In Melbourne's City Square, a large crowd heard Gough at his most belligerent. All this was done to the campaign slogan 'Shame Fraser Shame'. *(Courtesy of The Age)*

Support from behind. There was no middle ground in one of the most volatile election campaigns ever fought in Australian history. Here Gough meets supporters at a park in Sydney's beachside suburb of Bronte. (*Courtesy of The Whitlam Institute and Robert Pearce/Fairfaxphotos*)

From Blacktown's Civic Centre to the Opera House. At Blacktown the stars were the cheer squad on the civic centre floor. Eighteen months later they were on the platform at the Opera House. Among those urging a vote for Labor were a surf champion, an artist, a soccer coach, an actress, an Aboriginal activist and the nation's best-known author, Nobel Prize-winner Patrick White. On 24 November 1975, in a campaign address in Melbourne, Gough told the nation: 'The decision you make on 13 December goes far beyond who will govern Australia for a few months or a few years. It goes to the heart of how Australia will be governed into the twenty-first century … The shame of the past six weeks must be wiped away. In those shameful six weeks, a stacked Senate went on strike against a Budget vital to Australia's welfare and the nation's economy. The nation and the nation's elected government was held to ransom. And by those means, the elected government in full command of the confidence of the Australian Parliament was deposed. Is Australia to continue to be a parliamentary democracy? Are we to have governments elected by the people, through the people's house? Are elected governments to govern? These are the questions. Upon the answer you give depends survival of parliamentary democracy as we know it—or as we believed we knew it until 11 November 1975. Remember that day. Mr Fraser's day of shame—a day that will live in infamy.' *(Courtesy of News Limited)*

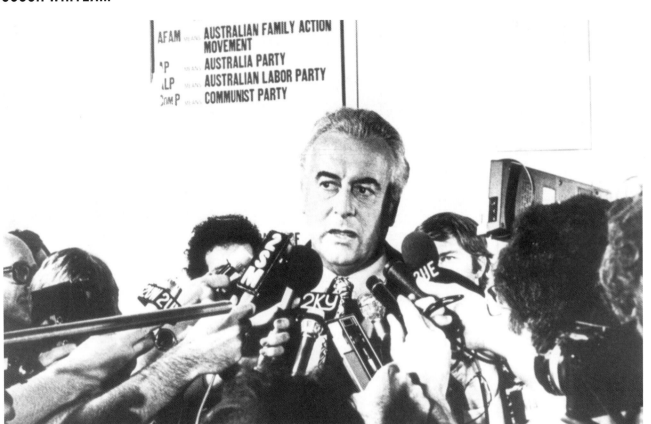

The end. At 11 pm on 15 December 1975, Gough concedes defeat. 'Let me just say how much my colleagues and I appreciate the magnificent spirit shown by the Labor movement during the last couple of months. I'd like to express in particular my profound regret at losing so many colleagues who were in the prime of their political life, and whose contribution to this country's political life has been interrupted.' *(Courtesy of the Canberra Times)*

From lodge to lodger. Malcom Fraser moved into the Lodge from the Commonwealth Club. Gough moved from the Lodge into a $19.70 a week government flat. *(Courtesy of Fairfaxphotos)*

Stand up and be counted. Soon after Malcolm Fraser's victory, Gough was presented with a manifesto from supporters at a rally in Collingwood, Melbourne. *(Courtesy of The Age)*

On his sixtieth birthday. Barely six months into the first Fraser government, Gough took the opportunity to remind the electorate of the difficulties presented by those ministers in his government whose behaviour 'has helped to get us out'. Although he vowed to lead Labor back to the office at the next election, he also admitted to having gone through 'a very bad patch' earlier in the year. *(Courtesy of The Age)*

TOKYO   35/33   31   0306

EDITOR MELBOURNE AGE SPENCER STREET,

MELBOURNE.

MY WIFE AND I ARE MUCH MOVED BY CARTOON OF

''THE AGE'' ALREADY ACCLAIMED AS CARTOON OF

THE YEAR —— MAY WE WITHOUT PREJUDICE HAVE

THE ORIGINAL?

...GOUGH WHITLAM.

Great movements. Peter Nicholson's cartoon of Gough and Margaret, who were in Tianjin, China, at the time of a massive earthquake, outraged many of the *The Age*'s readers. The Great Man, however, was appropriately amused by Nicholson's speculations on his and Margaret's marital conversations. *(Courtesy of Peter Nicholson)*

The veterans. On the first anniversary of the Dismissal, Gough joined family and friends to celebrate his becoming the longest serving federal leader of the Labor Party, a run of nine years, nine months and four days. On his retirement from the leadership on the day of the second Fraser victory in 1977, Gough had served a total of ten years, a Labor record yet to be surpassed. In the picture from the front left are Michael Delaney, Fred Daly, Margaret, Evan Williams, Tony Whitlam, Richard Whitington, Lorraine Dwyer, Gough, Ros Byrne, Graham Freudenberg and Bill Pinwill. *(Courtesy of the Canberra Times)*

My best appointment. Gough and Margaret, a rock-solid duo, dance the 'Anniversary Waltz' at the Sutherland Civic Centre in November 1977 to mark Gough's 25 years in politics. *(Courtesy of News Limited)*

The next Labor PM. ALP president Bob Hawke and Gough confer during the party's 1977 national conference. Hawke's moderate response to the Dismissal, which damped down calls for widespread industrial action, demonstrated his influence within the party. *(Courtesy of The Age)*

Another tough campaign. After a year of speculation about the leadership of the party and a leadership spill, which he survived, Gough went into the 1977 election portrayed by the Coalition as Labor's major electoral liablility. At the Opera House campaign launch on 17 November one reporter noted that Gough had lost his magic and that his low key manner garnered a flat reaction from the audience. His address, however, looked brilliant on TV. *(Courtesy of Fairfaxphotos)*

The last supper. On the evening before the 1977 election, Gough joined his family (pictured) and staff in Sydney's Chinatown for dinner. His message in the last days of the campaign was a warning that Coalition promises were based on 'the crudest appeal to greed'. *(Courtesy of David Bartho/Fairfaxphotos)*

The end had come. As he toured the 44 booths in his huge western suburbs electorate of Werriwa in the blazing heat of election day, Gough knew that if the Labor Party lost he would retire to the backbench. The results came in and the Coalition was returned with its huge majority almost unaltered. At 11.16 pm on Saturday 10 December 1977 Gough told the Australian people with great dignity that he would not be nominating for the position of leader of the Australian Labor Party. *(Courtesy of the Whitlam Institute)*

On the backbench. On 22 December 1977, Bill Hayden (centre) replaced Gough as federal leader of the Labor Party. Gough adopted a low profile on the backbench. He rarely spoke or asked questions, but remained active outside the parliament giving speeches and addresses on issues that concerned him. On 14 July 1978, he announced his retirement after more than 25 years as the member for Werriwa. Here Gough joins Bill Hayden and the man who would be the next Labor prime minister, Bob Hawke. *(Courtesy of the Canberra Times)*

A vice-regal acknowledgement. In 1978 Sir John Kerr's successor, Sir Zelman Cowan, invested Gough with the Order of Australia. David Smith (centre), the Governor-General's secretary who had read the dismissal notice on the front steps of Parliament House, looks on. In less than three years Gough had gone from the 'order of the boot' to the Order of Australia. *(Courtesy of the Canberra Times)*

A long wait. In his maiden speech in 1952, Gough called for a large teaching hospital to be established in Sydney's rapidly growing western suburbs. He had to wait for a quarter of a century and three years of a Whitlam government before he was able to attend the opening ceremony of Westmead Hospital. *(Courtesy of News Limited)*

Generation(s) gap. Gough is left holding the baby at an art exhibition in Melbourne, April 1978. *(Courtesy of The Age)*

The happy salesman. Back on the campaign trail in 1979, this time to promote *The Truth of the Matter*. Gough's book was in answer to Sir John Kerr's *Matters for Judgement*, published the previous year. *(Courtesy of The Age)*

Four men and a prince. A less-than-impressed John Gorton, the seemingly genial duo of Gough and his successor Malcom Fraser, and Billy McMahon as courtiers during Prince Charles' visit to Australia in 1979. Gough, the republican, always held the Queen in genuine affection.*(Courtesy of News Limited)*

The fight goes on. From the day in 1975 when he handed back Gurindji land to Vincent Lingiari, Gough never wavered from his belief in Aboriginal self-determination. *(Courtesy of the Whitlam Institute)*

Gough and Nugget. H.C. 'Nugget' Coombes (right) was Gough's most trusted advisor on Aboriginal affairs. It was Nugget's last-minute suggestion that Gough pour the red Gurindji sand into Vincent Lingiari's hand. In 2001, Vincent's son Victor returned the symbolism by the pouring Gurindji soil into Gough's hand. *(Courtesy of the National Archives of Australia)*

An ongoing love affair. Affection for Gough has never waned. This birthday message was delivered at a land rights demonstration in Sydney in 1980. *(Courtesy of the Whitlam Institute)*

In 'retirement'. The years after Gough's departure from parliament were marked by growing regard for the old campaigner. His attendance at Labor events could spark enthusiasm reminiscent of the 1972 campaign. At a Melbourne 'Festival of Labor' in 1981 one supporter told Gough, 'Don't settle for second prize and be GG!' *(Courtesy of the Whitlam Institute)*

Against ignorance. In 1981, Liberal Treasurer John Howard proposed imposing a tax on books. This outraged historian Geoffrey Blainey who said it was like 'appointing a Minister for Ignorance'. Stephen Murray-Smith of the National Book Council suggested the tax was 'a reminder of the strength of puritanism in Australian life'. Gough joined senators Flo Bjelke-Petersen and Don Chipp in denouncing the proposal. *(Courtesy of The Age)*

Poisoned chalice. In 1982, Gough toured East Timor. *The Age* commentator Peter Hastings dryly remarked, 'Indonesians like him because he likes them, rather too uncritically perhaps'. Earlier, in 1977, Gough had provoked outrage when he contradicted Labor Party policy by suggesting that self-determination for East Timor was no longer feasible. *(Courtesy of The Age)*

Anything for a cause. Multiculturalism had some costs. Here Gough suffers at the hands of the irrepressible Al Grassby during the Sydney Festival del Sol in 1982. Gough had previously received the 'Order of the Poncho' in 1980. *(Courtesy of News Limited)*

Eternal enmity. Gough is watched over by Clifton Pugh's portrait of Sir John Kerr at a Melbourne book launch in 1981 before a crowd of 200 people, 'the biggest audience he had ever drawn in Toorak'. In 1972, Pugh won the Archibald Prize with a portrait of Gough. The Great Man sent the artist a telegram that began, 'My place in the history of art and yours in the history of politics are now secure'. *(Courtesy of The Age)*

Proud of his 'best appointment'. When Margaret Whitlam received an Order of Australia she mischievously remarked that Gough's response has been 'very appreciative'. 'He's inclined to suggest that it's almost my due.' Margaret once reminded an audience that the nation paid its prime minister a wage and got his wife's work free. *(Courtesy of News Limited)*

A royal gala. In 1982, nearly a decade after the first sod was turned, the National Gallery of Australia was finally opened by the Queen. Among those celebrating one of the Whitlam government's cultural legacies were Gough and Margaret, John and Bettina Gorton, and Sonia and Billy McMahon. *(Courtesy of the National Archives of Australia)*

Mr Ambassador. Gough and Margaret Whitlam with their grandson Edward Hugo Whitlam just after Bob Hawke announced Gough's appointment as Australia's ambassador to Unesco. From 1983 until 1986, Gough devoted his customary energy to preserving the world's natural and historical patrimony from further corrosion. *(Courtesy Robert Pearce/Fairfaxphotos)*

Three reformers. A month after Labor was returned to office under Bob Hawke, Gough joined his High Court appointment, Lionel Murphy, and the new Attorney-General, Gareth Evans, for the launch of *Australia's Constitution: Time for Change.* It was a theme close to Gough's heart. *(Courtesy of News Limited)*

In full flight. Almost a decade after the Dismissal, Gough had lost little of his energy and none of his will to evangelise. The National Press Club, where he was among friends and foes he had known for many years, was a congenial setting for his energies. As Michelle Grattan wrote in 1984: 'Gough Whitlam, his Excellency the Ambassador to Unesco, returned for the twelfth time to the National Press Club yesterday, and all of a sudden it was 1973 again...' When Mungo McCallum asked if Paris was as much fun as Australia used to be, Gough firmly replied, 'The fun is where I am'. *(Courtesy of the Canberra Times)*

THE
WHITLAM
GOVERNMENT
1972-1975

A publisher's delight. Gough poured the same enthusiasm that had characterised so much of his life into the promotion of each of his four books. Here he speaks at the launch of his magnum opus, a 798-page account of his government's record laced, of course, with his wicked wit. *(Courtesy of the Herald and Weekly Times)*

Paris and a bit of joie de champagne. Among Gough's closest friends in politics was Fred Daly, the genial leader of the House of Representatives from 1972–75. Remembering the chaos in Cabinet during the early days of the Whitlam government, Fred Daly commented: 'We'd hardly had a beer together when, all of a sudden, we were expected to run the country together.' *(Courtesy of the Whitlam Institute)*

Tea for two. In public E. G. Whitlam was rarely other than magisterial. Here the private Gough shares a cup of tea with his friend Tom Burns, who was at the time Queensland opposition leader. *(Courtesy of the Whitlam Institute)*

The camera loved Gough and the love was rewarded. In 1987, Gough became chair of the National Gallery of Australia. A few weeks before, he 'opened' the newly refurbished gallery shop where he was caught in a wistful moment in front of Colin McCahon's *Victory over Death II. (Courtesy of The Age)*

The Gough and John show. Sharing the opening of Old Parliament House as a museum with John Gorton, Gough chose to emulate Billy McMahon, the prime minister he dispatched. Gough once described McMahon as 'Tiberius with a telephone' in a reference to McMahon's efforts to unseat Gorton. For his part, Gorton chose to be photographed glass in hand, a reference perhaps to press reports of his easy familiarity with the bottle. *(Courtesy of the Canberra Times)*

Creating a good impression. As chairman of the National Gallery of Australia, Gough joined staff and friends in recreating a tableau of Renoir's *Luncheon of the Boating Party. (Courtesy of the Canberra Times)*

To catch a spy. When the British government attempted to prevent the publication in Australia of the memoirs of a retired espionage bureaucrat, the brouhaha was guaranteed entertainment for months as the matter proceeded through the courts. Here Peter Wright, the spycatcher, is flanked by his lawyer and now Liberal member of federal parliament, Malcom Turnbull, at the launch of Turnbull's book, *The Spycatcher Trial.* Gough, who described Wright 'as the one in the National Party hat', declared that 'Australian courts are better than British Courts'; the latter, like the British press, were 'sycophantic'. *(Courtesy of News Limited)*

Confucius says. One of the many posts the 'retired' ex-PM accepted was chair of the Australia–China Council. When asked by a female journalist whether he had ever considered being a Buddhist, Gough replied in mock horror, 'I don't talk about my religion to strange women'. *(Courtesy of The Age)*

Who would imagine that chairing an art gallery could be so much fun? Chairman Gough donned a purple toga and gold-leaf garland to announce that the British Museum would be sending a large collection of antiquities to the National Gallery of Australia. Originally, it was suggested that Gough would walk across water, to which he replied: 'Comrade, that would not have been possible—the stigmata have not yet healed.' *(Courtesy of the Canberra Times)*

A friend returns. Gough's first contact with the original Australians was at Gove in the Northern Territory in 1943, where he was posted by the RAAF. Forty-eight years later he is pictured among friends gathered in a rocky creek bed 600 kilometres southwest of Darwin to mark the 25th anniversary of the stockmen's strike at Wave Hill. Led by Vincent Lingiari, that strike was the start of the modern land rights movement. *(Courtesy of News Limited)*

Return season? As undergraduates both Gough and Margaret appeared behind the footlights. Five decades later, they played at the Melbourne Concert Hall in the Edith Sitwell and William Walton extravaganza *Façade*. *(Courtesy of the Herald and Weekly Times)*

Keeping in touch. Older, wiser but with no less enthusiasm, Gough reflects on the Hawke–Keating contest and the meaning of leadership at the launch of his old comrade Fred Daly's political discovery map of Canberra. 'Presumably I have been given the distinction and pleasure of launching Fred Daly's political map,' he said, 'because I am the only surviving small-town Australian politician to have become prime minister. When I was brought here by my parents in 1928 Canberra was ... sheep country (flies) with a continental climate (chillbains). I early became accustomed to walking across Lake Burley Griffin. The map reveals that I did not come from a log cabin, but a mock Tudor house.' *(Courtesy of the Canberra Times)*

Life membership. After more than forty years of service to the Labor Party, Gough was finally given life membership by the NSW party in 1992 to the rapturous applause of delegates at the State Conference. Fifteen years later, in 2007, Gough and Margaret were made life members of the national party. *(Courtesy of Kate Callas/Fairfaxphotos)*

Old foes with a common cause. In 1991, Malcolm Fraser and Gough Whitlam led the protests against Kerry Packer's bid with Conrad Black for control of Fairfax. Among the protesting crowds would have been many stringent critics of both former leaders. *(Courtesy of the Canberra Times)*

True believers. Paul Keating served as Minister for Northern Australia for barely three weeks in the final days of the Whitlam government. On arriving in parliament as a new chum in 1969, he was advised by Gough to get himself a university degree. 'What! And end up like you?' was the Bankstown boy's riposte. *(Courtesy of News Limited)*

A republican cause. Gough's first tussle with the Constitution was over John Curtin's campaign to realign federal and state responsibilities in 1944. In 1992, the issue was the republic. The old warhorse was utterly at home during the Great Republic Debate held in Old Parliament House. *(Courtesy of News Limited)*

Another anniversary celebration. Patricia Amphlett, better known as Little Pattie, and 'the Labor superman who fell but never faded away' relive the birth of 'It's Time' twenty years later at an Adelaide anniversary dinner. *(Courtesy of News Limited)*

Surrounded by rubbery figures. Gough Whitlam casts a stern eye over Bill Hayden, Malcolm Fraser and Paul Keating at the launch of an exhibition of cartoonist Peter Nicholson's work. He reminded those present that the words 'rubbery figures' had once been used by the Liberal Phillip Lynch to describe one of Gough's budgets and that Liberal leader John Hewson had divulged that Gough had introduced AIDS to Australia—Acquired Income Dependency Syndrome. *(Courtesy of The Age)*

School reunion, class of 1973. Twenty years after the formation of the third Whitlam Cabinet (the first was the Whitlam/Barnard duumvirate), some of the survivors meet up again. Among the faces: Al Grassby, Kep Enderby, Ken Wriedt, Les Johnson, Lance Barnard, Joe Riordon, Frank Crean and Paul Keating. *(Courtesy of the Sydney Morning Herald)*

'And the winner is Sideney'. Gough and Margaret played an important role in Sydney's successful bid to host the 2000 Olympics. Without Gough's courting of the African vote, the city would not have held the 'best Olympics ever'. *(Courtesy of the Whitlam Institute)*

Labor mythology. The stories and legends that accompanied the birth of the Labor Party in the 1890s remain a durable part of its identity, despite the passage of time and the transformations of Australian society. Barcaldine in outback Queensland has a strong claim to being the birthplace of Labor. In 1993, Gough made a pilgrimage to the historic site via the railway station at Emerald where, with bell in hand, he summoned passengers to board the train to Barcaldine. *(Courtesy of The Age)*

Still making headlines. Gough at a National Press Club lunch to mark the 20th anniversary of the Dismissal. *(Courtesy of the Canberra Times)*

Line of succession. Gough (Werriwa 1952–78) and John Kerin (Werriwa 1978–93) greet Mark Latham (Werriwa 1993–2005). In 1993, Gough could see only great things ahead for Mark Latham, his favourite son of the Labor Party. Twelve years later he could offer no solace when Latham led the ALP to a devastating defeat in the 2005 federal election. Later, Latham denounced his friendship with his mentor. *(Courtesy of News Limited)*

Birthday bash. On his 80th birthday on 11 July 1996, Gough cuts a cake at the State Library of NSW where he marked the occasion by launching Barry Cohen's *Life With Gough*, a selection of anecdotes that captured the 'leader's' indomitable spirit. The cake's Latin inscription reads 'Growing Old with Grace'. The next day the *Australian*'s editorial reminded readers that 'At 80, Mr Whitlam still maintains a punishing schedule. His wit is still sharp; his intellect still searching and his political beliefs as constant as ever ... Even his political enemies have softened. The nation has much to appreciate in the long productive life of E.G. Whitlam.' *(Courtesy of News Limited)*

Legal minds, all. Gough joined Mr Justice Michael Kirby of the High Court and former NSW premier Neville Wran at the Lionel Murphy Memorial Lecture. How to deal with the mercurial Senator Murphy had been a longstanding issue during Gough's prime ministership. In Februrary 1975, Gough appointed Murphy to the High Court of Australia. Murphy's brilliant legal mind and his great compassion could not save him from the bad judgement that blotted his political and judicial career. *(Courtesy of the Canberra Times)*

From derision to asset. In 1973 Prime Minister Gough Whitlam provoked outrage when he authorised the National Gallery of Australia to purchase Jackson Pollock's *Blue Poles* for $A1.34 million. A quarter of a century later, and thought to be worth between $100 and $150 million, Gough welcomed its return from a tour of the Tate in London and the Museum of Modern Art in New York with a mischievious recounting of the views of those who'd condemned the purchase. *(Courtesy of The Age)*

Gough and The Whitlams. The musical ones are on their knees in mock obeisance as their namesake presents them with the Band of the Year Award at the 1998 ARIA awards. *(Courtesy of News Limited)*

A rich life. After nearly seventy years of marriage, Margaret Whitlam was one of Gough's greatest admirers and sharpest critics. She was his *prima donna*. Here she stands besides Clifton Pugh's prime ministerial portrait. *(Courtesy of Rick Stevens/Fairfaxphotos)*

GOUGH WHITLAM

In full flight. Gough retained the joy of battle and was always prepared to turn an enthusiasm into a campaign. When those who believed the Parthenon Marbles should be restored to their original place wanted an articulate, erudite champion, they turned to Gough. *(Courtesy of the Canberra Times)*

The Whitlam legacy. The man whose prime ministership was the most controversial in Australia's history changed the country forever. His belief in ideas and public service for the greater good continued beyond the three years of his government. Margaret, who had been Gough's enduring companion, who had sustained and supported him, died aged 92 on 17 March 2012. Gough died on 21 October 2014. His light will never diminish. *(Courtesy of the Whitlam Institute)*

SOURCES

In compiling the captions we have drawn on the texts that accompanied them on first publication and on a collection of remarkably high-quality writings prompted by Gough Whitlam's public successes and failures. Whatever one's final judgement on his achievements, his impact on the calibre of political writing in Australia is undeniable.

Barry Cohen   *Life With Gough*
                               Allen & Unwin, 1996

Graham Freudenberg   *A Certain Grandeur: Gough Whitlam in Politics*
                               Macmillan, 1977

John Menadue   *Things You Learn Along the Way*
                               David Lovell Publishing, 1999

Laurie Oakes   *Whitlam, PM*
                               Angus & Robertson, 1973

Michael Sexton   *Illusions of Power: The Fate of a Reform Government*
                               Allen & Unwin, 1979

James Walter   *The Leader*
                               University of Queensland Press, 1980

Gough Whitlam   *The Truth of the Matter*
                               Penguin, 1983

Gough Whitlam   *The Whitlam Government*
                               Penguin, 1985

Gough Whitlam   *Abiding Interests*
                               University of Queensland Press, 1997

Gough Whitlam   *My Italian Notebook*
                               Allen & Unwin, 2002